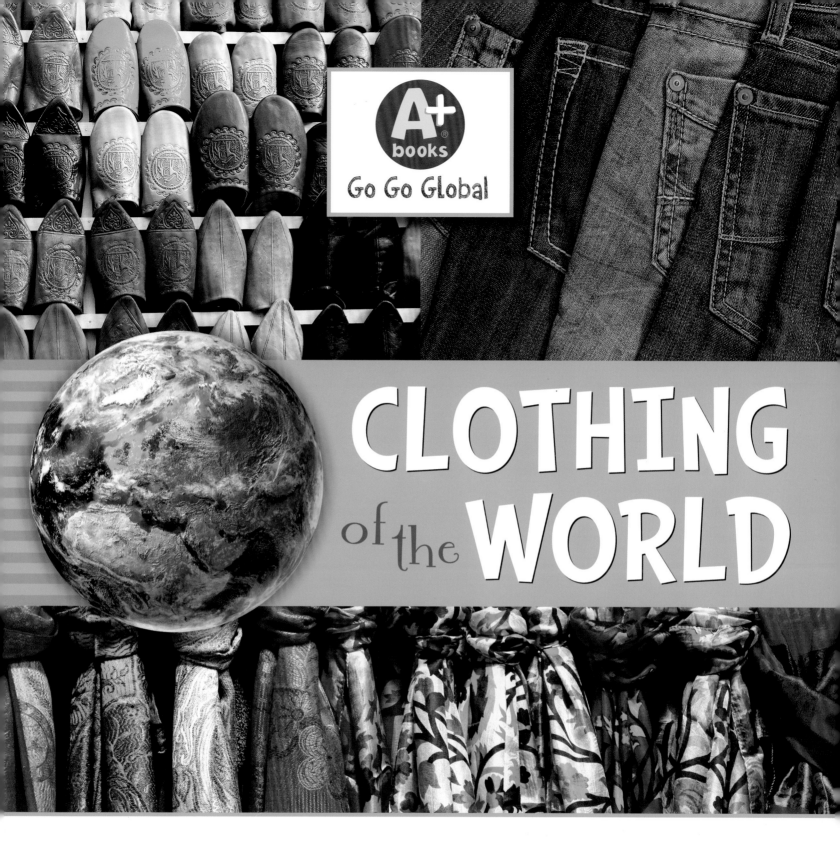

A+ books
Go Go Global

CLOTHING
of the WORLD

by Nancy Loewen and Paula Skelley

raintree
a Capstone company — publishers for children

Hats, coats, trousers and skirts ...

Peru

shoes, shorts,

Cuba

Pakistan

South Africa

Indonesia

shawls and shirts –

3

from the
tops
of our
heads

Russia

Poland

to the **tips** of our **toes,**

around the world

India

we all wear clothes.

Hats for work,

United States

Benin

Scotland

Mongolia

hats for celebrations ...

Ukraine

hats for warmth,

Vietnam

hats for shade,

Norway

India

Colombia

hats for **special** occasions.

9

India

Now let's see what's on our feet,

United States

Tanzania

protecting us from **cold** and **heat.**

Ethiopia

Slip
them **on.**

Tie the
laces.

United States

12

Ready, shoes?

New Zealand

Let's go places!

Off to school!

Mexico

Germany

India

What will YOU wear?

China

A **shirt** with a **collar**
or a **dress** with a **flare?**

Will you **put on** a
jumper?

Ireland

Vietnam

How about
a **tie?**

Whatever you wear,

United States

wear school clothes with pride.

Time to play!

Ethiopia

China

Let's have some fun –

18

in the
rain

Ukraine

or
in the
sun.

Canada 19

England

Play in water ...

Australia

Bulgaria

play in **snow** ...

Burundi

run so **fast** ...

go, go, **go!**

Tanzania

Argentina

Some **clothes** have a **special** mission:

Czech Republic

Russia

to **honour** the **past** and **show** **tradition**.

Beads and feathers ...

United States

China

Japan

silks and
bows ...

clothes

here and **now** ...

Spain

China

from long **ago.**

NORTH
AMERICA

Canada

United
States

Mexico

Cuba

Colombia

Peru

SOUTH
AMERICA

Argentina

Norway

Scotland

England

Ireland

Germany

Spain

EUROPE

Poland

Ukraine

Czech Republic

Bulgaria

Pakistan

AFRICA

Benin

Ethiopia

Burundi

Tanzania

South
Africa

ANTARCTICA

Russia

ASIA

Mongolia

Japan

China

India

●—Vietnam

Indonesia

AUSTRALIA
Australia

New Zealand

GLOSSARY

celebration activities that mark a special day

collar band or strap worn around the neck

flare spreading outwards at the bottom

honour give praise or show respect

mission planned job or task

occasion special or important event

pride feeling that one has worth and importance

protect keep safe

shawl piece of soft material that is worn over the shoulders or around the head

tradition custom, idea or belief passed down over time

GO GO GLOBAL DISCUSSION QUESTIONS

1. Name three reasons why a person might wear a hat.

2. Which clothes in this book are most like yours? Which clothes are least like yours? How are they different?

3. Look at the clothes in the Cultural section. Explain how they are different from play clothes or school clothes.

Raintree is an imprint of Capstone Global Library Limited, a company incorporated in England and Wales having its registered office at 7 Pilgrim Street, London, EC4V 6LB – Registered company number: 6695582

www.raintree.co.uk
myorders@raintree.co.uk

Edited by Jill Kalz
Designed by Juliette Peters
Picture research by Tracy Cummins
Production by Tori Abraham
Printed and bound in China.

ISBN 978 1 474 70368 0
19 18 17 16 15
10 9 8 7 6 5 4 3 2 1

British Library Cataloguing in Publication Data
A full catalogue record for this book is available from the British Library.

Acknowledgements
Alamy: Michele and Tom Grimm, 11 Left; Shutterstock: Alena Ozerova, 19 Top, Alexandra Lande, 14 Bottom, Andrea Obzerova, 4 Bottom, Andresr, 17, Andy Dean Photography, 14 TL, Anton_Ivanov, 6 BL, 12 Top, 18 Top, aphotostory, 27 Top, aslysun, 18 Bottom, bikeriderlondon, Cover BR, Dasha Petrenko, 13, De Visu, 4 Top, Digital Media Pro, 26, Distinctive Images, 3 BR, Filip Fuxa, Cover TL, Goran Bogicevic, 2, ISchmidt, 19 Bottom, Jeanne Provost, 6 Top, Kanokratnok, 11 Right, 24 TL, katatonia82, 1 Bottom, kolo5, 16 Top, Lam Tom, Cover Back, leocalvett, Cover, 1, (Globe), ludmilafoto, 1 TR, Mikadun, 1 TL, 10, Monkey Business Images, 15, 20 Top, Nagy-Bagoly Arpad, 12 Bottom, NigelSpiers, 8 Bottom, Ninelle, 28, Nolte Lourens, Cover TR, 3 BL, OlegD, 9 BL, Pablo Rogat, 5, Paolo Bona, 6 BR, R.M. Nunes, Cover BL, racorn, 14 TR, Rafal Cichawa, 9 Right, Robyn Butler, 20 Bottom, Sergey Novikov, 21, Sokolova Maryna, 8 Top, Stawek, 30, sunsinger, 24 TR, Vladimir Wrangel, 24 Bottom, withGod, 7, 25, XiXinXing, 29, Zzvet, 3 TR; SuperStock: age fotostock, 27 Bottom, Charles O. Cecil/age fotostock, 3 TL, Robert Harding Picture Library, 9 TL, Travel Pix Collection/Jon Arnold Images, 16 Bottom, Walter Zerla/age fotostock, 22 Bottom.

Every effort has been made to contact copyright holders of material reproduced in this book. Any omissions will be rectified in subsequent printings if notice is given to the publisher.

BOOKS

Clothes Around the World (Around the World), Clare Lewis (Raintree, 2015)

Clothing (Our Global Community), Lisa Easterling (Raintree, 2008)

Play (Say What You See), Rebecca Rissman (Raintree, 2013)

WEBSITES

www.bbc.co.uk/schools/barnabybear/
Travel the world with Barnaby Bear.

www.britishmuseum.org/channel/kids/young_explorers_videos/video_a_history_of_clothing.aspx
Watch this video about the history of clothing.